Contents

How to use this book

Each page has a title telling you what it is about.

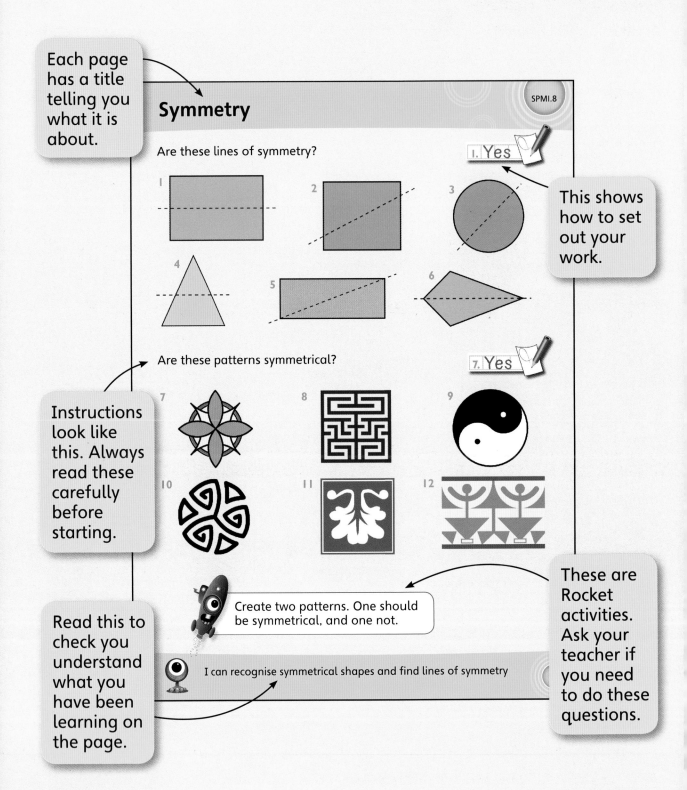

Symmetry

Are these lines of symmetry?

1.
2.
3.

1. Yes

This shows how to set out your work.

4.
5.
6.

Are these patterns symmetrical?

7. Yes

Instructions look like this. Always read these carefully before starting.

7.
8.
9.

10.
11.
12.

These are Rocket activities. Ask your teacher if you need to do these questions.

Create two patterns. One should be symmetrical, and one not.

Read this to check you understand what you have been learning on the page.

I can recognise symmetrical shapes and find lines of symmetry

3D objects

Look at these pictures.
Which show shapes that are:

1. a, d, ...

cuboids?

pyramids?

cylinders?

cones?

Which shapes have flat faces?

Which shapes have curved faces?

Which shapes could you use to print a circle? How about a square?

 I can recognise and name 3D objects

3

3D objects

Look at the pictures.
Which show shapes with:

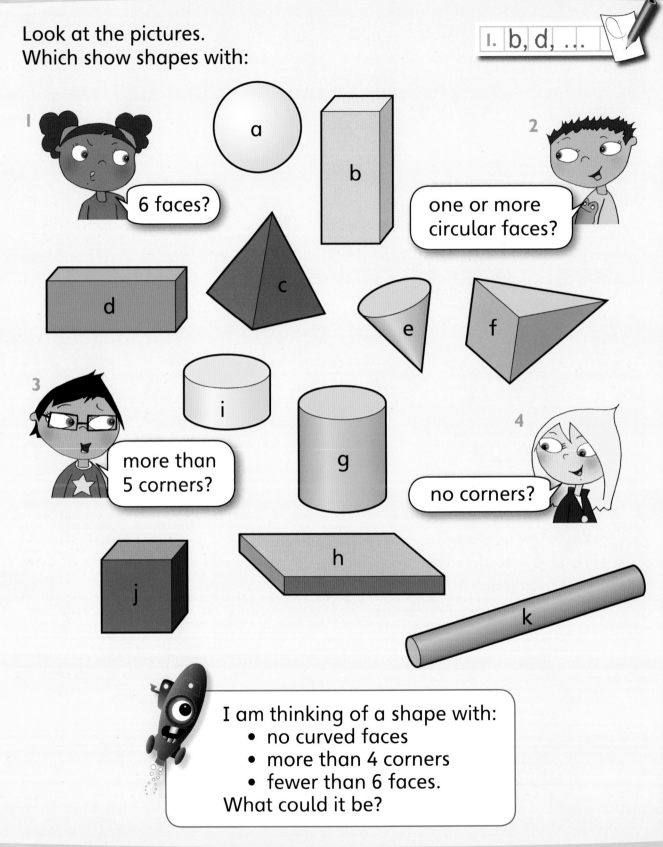

I. b, d, ...

a

b

6 faces?

one or more circular faces?

d

c

e

f

more than 5 corners?

i

g

no corners?

j

h

k

I am thinking of a shape with:
- no curved faces
- more than 4 corners
- fewer than 6 faces.
What could it be?

 I can recognise and name 3D objects

3D objects

1   These pictures show different objects.
Use the words to help you write the shape of each object.

cube   cuboid   cylinder   cone   pyramid   sphere

a   b   c   d   e

BEANS   CORNFLAKES

f   g   h   i

choc mints

2   Look at the objects above.
Write how many:

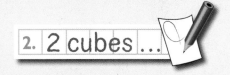

2. 2 cubes ...

cubes	cuboids	pyramids	cones
cylinders	prisms	spheres	

For each shape, write the number of:
faces   vertices   edges

I can recognise and name 3D objects

5

Flat and curved faces

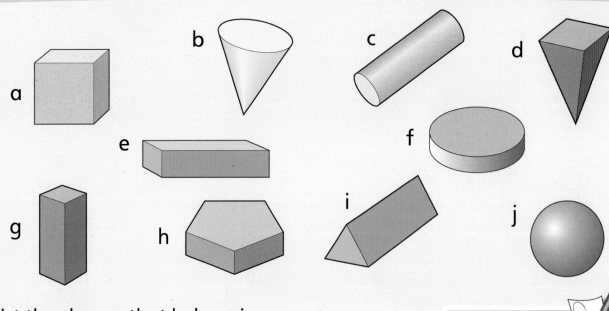

List the shapes that belong in:

1. a, d, ...

1 the red section

2 the blue section

3 the yellow section

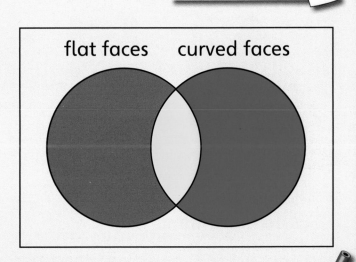

flat faces   curved faces

Which of the shapes have:

4 no flat faces   5 two curved faces   4. j

6 no curved faces   7 six flat faces

8 one curved face   9 five flat faces

Invent your own way of sorting some 3D objects but keep it secret. Can your partner work out how you sorted them?

I can talk about the properties of 3D objects

Sides

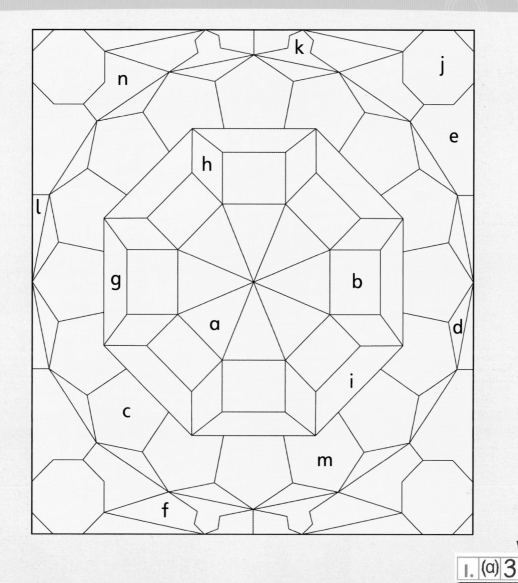

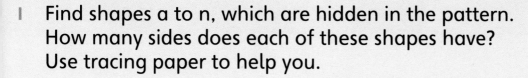

1 Find shapes a to n, which are hidden in the pattern.
   How many sides does each of these shapes have?
   Use tracing paper to help you.

2 List the shapes which are: triangles; pentagons; hexagons.

Make a pattern of your own with straight
lines. Can you find any triangles in it?
What other shapes can you find?

  I can say the names of 2D shapes

2D shapes

1 Choose any two shapes below. Write one **similarity** and one **difference** between them. Colour does not count.

> I chose shapes d and e. Similarity, they are both triangles; difference, e has sides all the same length and d doesn't.

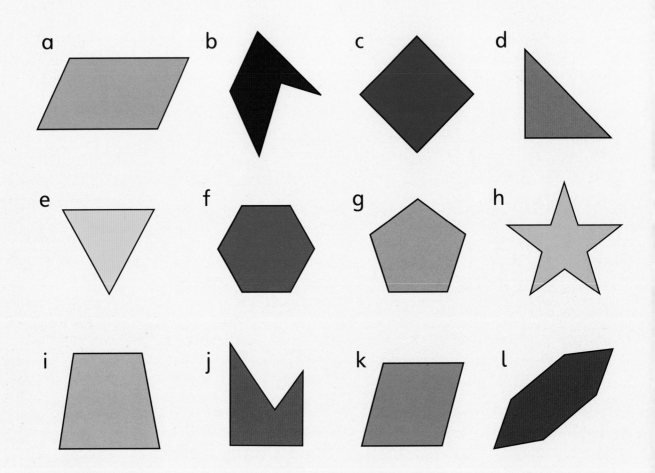

2 Repeat for 5 different pairs of shapes.

Choose a property of 2D shapes. Put counters on all the shapes on this page which share this property. Can your partner guess the property?

I can recognise similarities and differences between 2D shapes

Joining shapes

1 Jo has some regular pentagon tiles.
She fits them together and uses another shaped
tile to fill the gaps. Which of these tiles could she use?

a    b   c 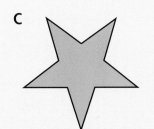   d

2 Jim has some regular octagon tiles.
He fits them together and uses another shaped tile
to fill the gaps. Which of the tiles below could he use?

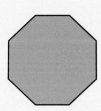

e 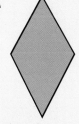   f   g 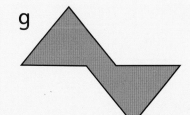   h

3 Josh has some regular hexagon tiles. He could fit
them together without gaps but chooses not to. He
uses other shaped tiles to fill the gaps. What could
those shapes be?

Choose any shape. Fit several of them together
and leave gaps on purpose. What kind of shapes
are the gaps you create?

 I can tile shapes and talk about the gaps between them

Tiling templates

Follow these instructions to make your own tessellating shape.

1 Start with any cardboard shape that tessellates.

2 Cut a shape from one side.

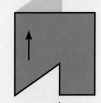

3 Slide the cut-out piece to the opposite side.

4 Stick the pieces together.

5 Now draw around your new shape to make tiling patterns.

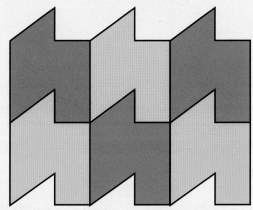

6 Is there just one way to make tiling patterns with your shape? Or more than one way?

Try the same thing with a more complicated shape. Or try cutting out a curved piece.

I can make shapes that tessellate

Symmetry

Are these lines of symmetry?

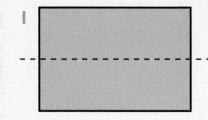
1

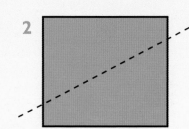
2

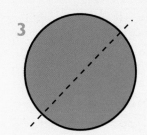
3

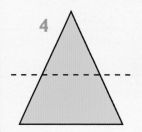
4

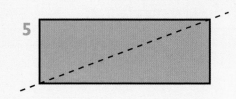
5

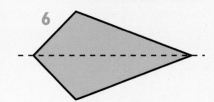
6

Are these patterns symmetrical?

7

8

9

10

11

12

Create two patterns. One should be symmetrical, and one not.

Symmetrical patterns

Use squared paper. Copy and complete
these symmetrical patterns.

1.

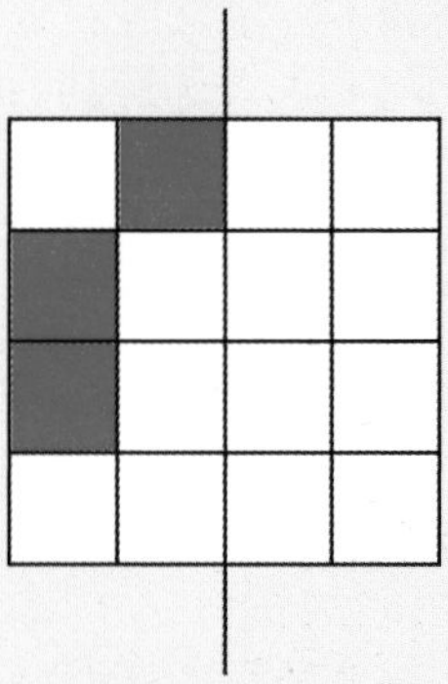

1

2

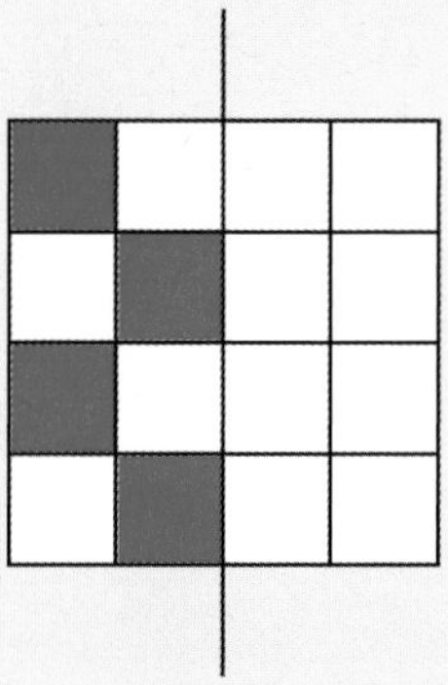

3

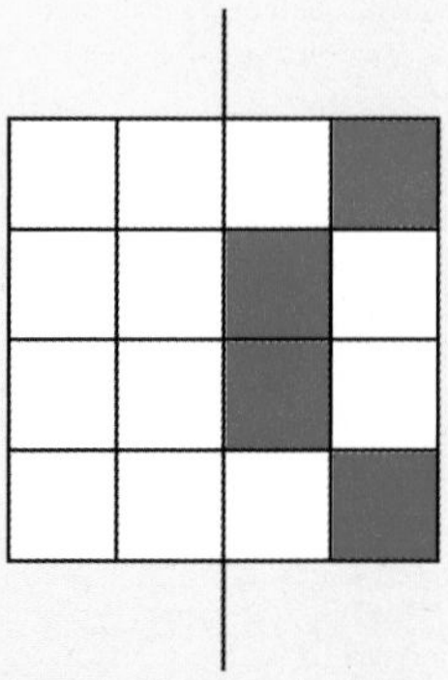

4

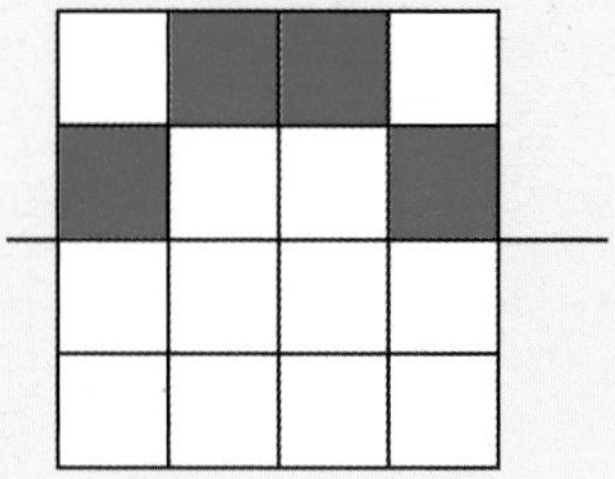

5

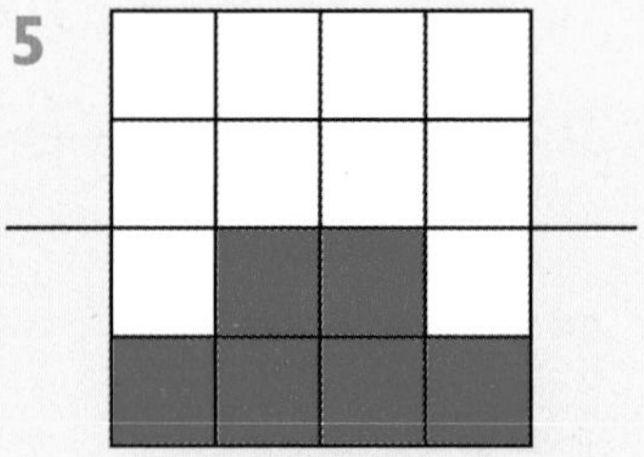

6

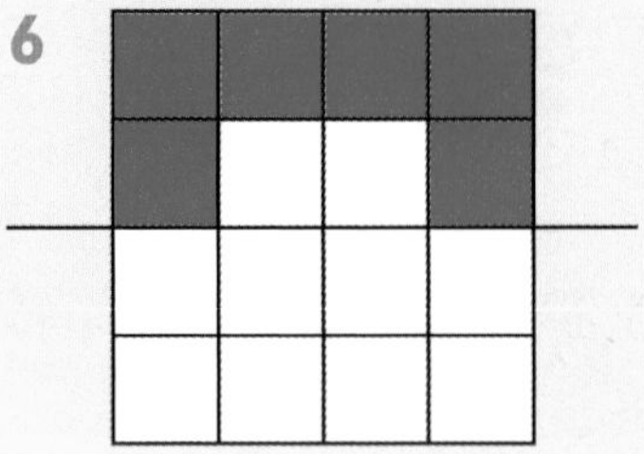

7

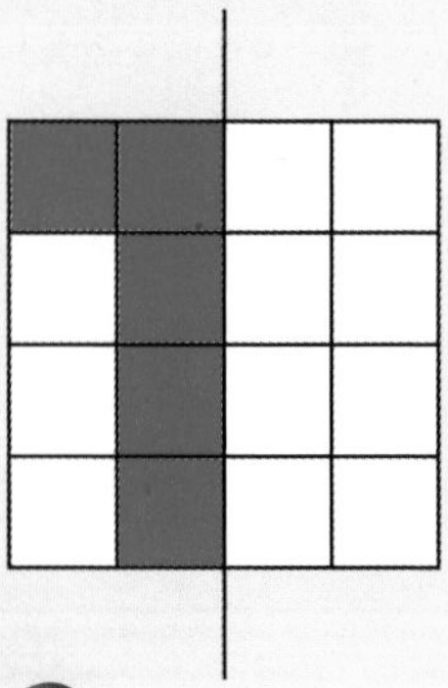

8

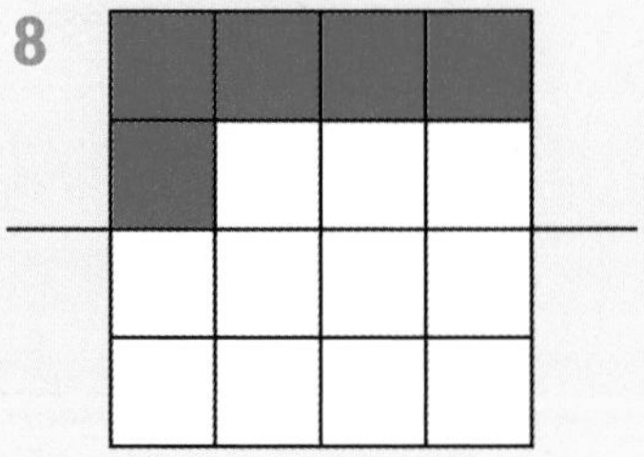

9

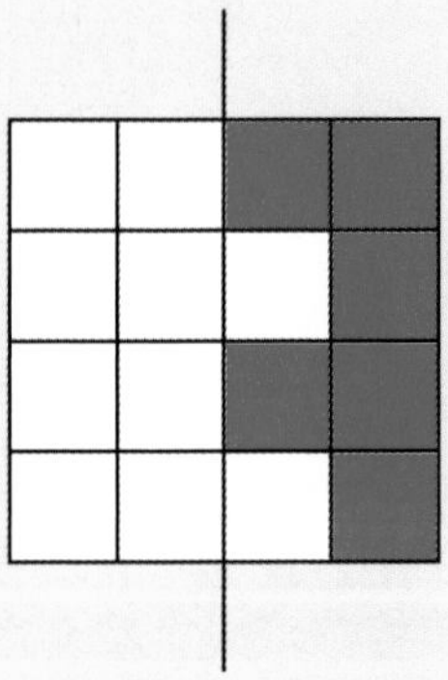

Use a grid of 16 squares like this but
with bigger squares, and draw a line of
symmetry from corner to corner. Start
off a symmetrical pattern using counters.
Ask your partner to complete the pattern.

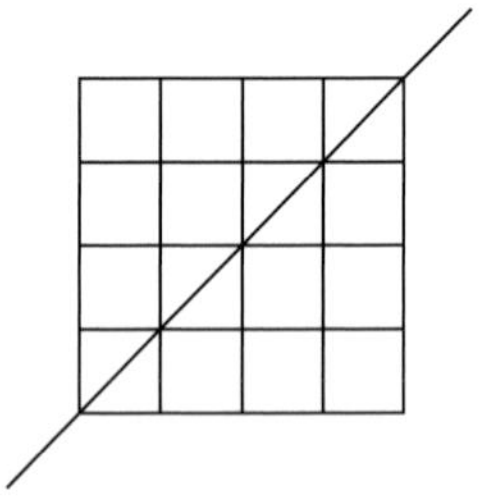

I can complete symmetrical patterns

Symmetry

Are these symmetrical patterns – yes or no?

1

2

3

4

5

6

Copy each picture. Draw the other half to create a symmetrical pattern.

7.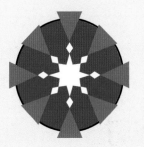

7

8

9

10

11

12

Find something symmetrical in the room. Sketch half of it.

 I can recognise and complete symmetrical patterns

13

Position

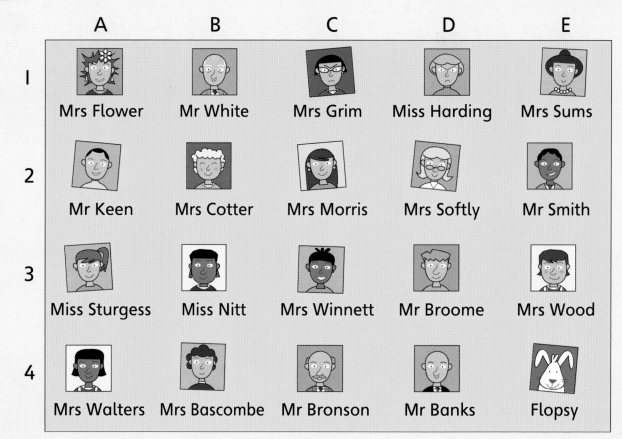

	A	B	C	D	E
1	Mrs Flower	Mr White	Mrs Grim	Miss Harding	Mrs Sums
2	Mr Keen	Mrs Cotter	Mrs Morris	Mrs Softly	Mr Smith
3	Miss Sturgess	Miss Nitt	Mrs Winnett	Mr Broome	Mrs Wood
4	Mrs Walters	Mrs Bascombe	Mr Bronson	Mr Banks	Flopsy

Write the position of these photographs:

1. C2

1 Mrs Morris   2 Mr Banks   3 Mr Smith

4 Miss Harding   5 Mr White   6 Mrs Walters

7 Mrs Softly   8 Mr Broome   9 Mrs Flower

Whose photographs are at these positions?

10 E1   11 A2   12 C3   13 E4   14 B2   15 C1

Look at a photograph. Tell your partner the position. Can they tell you who it is? Take turns at guessing.

I can describe a position within a grid

Position

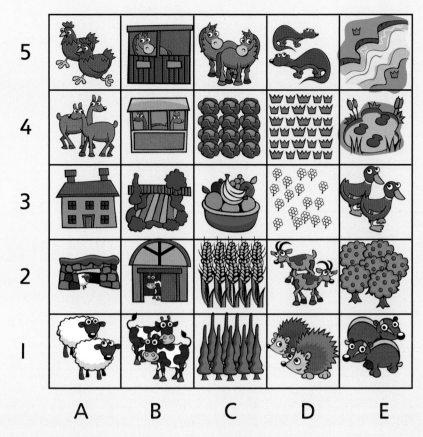

Describe the position of these animals:

1 chickens	2 hedgehogs	3 badgers	4 ducks
5 otters	6 horses	7 sheep	8 cows

What do the pictures at these positions show?

9 B2   10 A3   11 D2   12 E5   13 E2   14 D3

15 Which animals are in column D?

Work with your partner to draw your own grid. Take turns to tell each other what to draw and which square to put it in. For example: 'Draw a rocket in F5'.

I can describe and find positions within a grid

Position

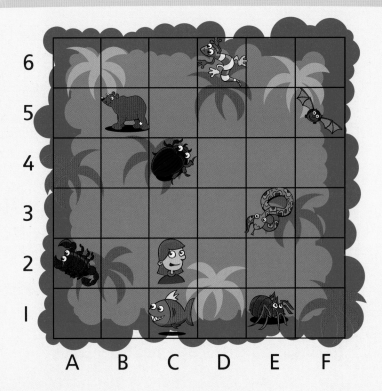

Tell Anna where the scary creatures are!
Give the position of:

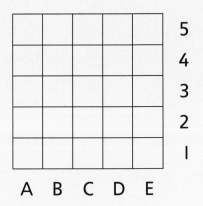

1 python   2 bear   3 spider   4 bat

5 scorpion   6 piranha   7 beetle   8 lizard

Draw 3 grids like this. On each grid, make
a letter of the alphabet by shading in
these positions:

9   B1, B2, B3, B4, B5, C3, D1, D2, D3, D4, D5

10 A1, A2, A3, A4, A5, B3, B5, C5, B1, C1

11 B1, B2, B3, B4, C4, C1, D1, D2, D3, D4

You need a 6 × 6 grid and a dice.
Invent a dice game to play on the grid.

I can describe and find positions within a grid

Making turns

Sam stands in his room. He follows each set of instructions.

What does he end up facing each time?

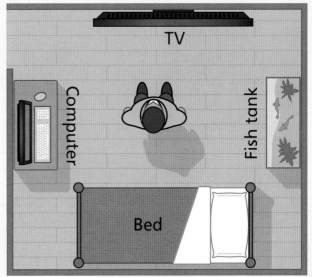

TV
Computer
Fish tank
Bed

1 Face the TV. Turn anticlockwise through a quarter turn.

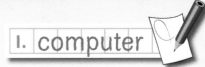

1. computer

2 Face the TV. Turn clockwise through a quarter turn.

3 Face the bed. Turn anticlockwise through a half turn.

4 Face the bed. Turn clockwise through a quarter turn.

5 Face the computer. Turn clockwise through a half turn.

6 Face the fish tank. Turn clockwise through a quarter turn.

7 Face the bed. Turn anticlockwise through three-quarters of a turn.

Make up two instructions for Sam. For example: 'Face the computer. Turn clockwise through a quarter turn. Then turn anticlockwise through a half turn.' Can your partner work out where Sam ends up facing?

I can understand instructions about turns

17

Routes

Follow each set of instructions and write the letter you end on:

1 Start at w, facing the stork. Go forwards 2 squares. Turn anticlockwise through a quarter turn. Go forwards 2 squares.

2 Start at u, facing the stork. Go forwards 1 square. Turn anticlockwise through a quarter turn. Go forwards 4 squares.

3 Start at k, facing the stork. Turn through a half turn. Go forwards 2 squares. Make a half turn. Go forwards 4 squares.

4 Start at j, facing the stork. Turn clockwise through a quarter turn. Go forwards 2 squares. Turn anticlockwise through a quarter turn. Go forwards 3 squares.

Make up sets of instructions like these for your partner to work out.

I can follow routes involving clockwise and anticlockwise turns

Cube models

Use cubes to build each shape.
How many faces does each shape have?

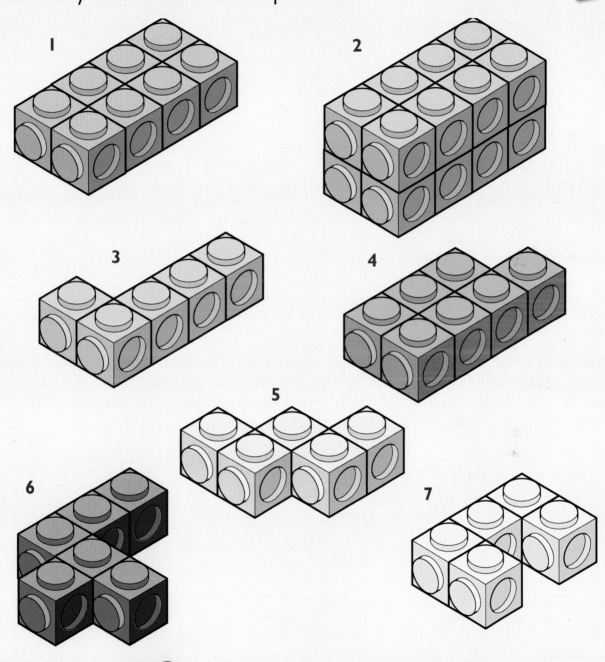

1

2

3

4

5

6

7

Make some shapes with 10 faces.

Quadrilaterals

Are these quadrilaterals?

1. Yes

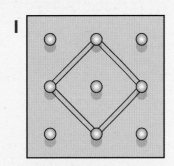
1

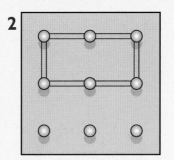
2

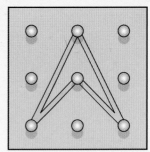
3

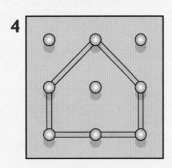
4

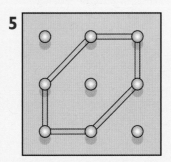
5

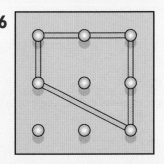
6

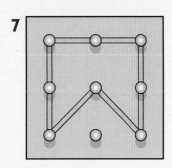
7

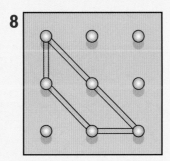
8

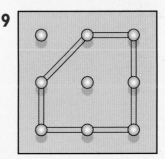
9

10 Write the names of the shapes that are not quadrilaterals.

11 Explore different quadrilaterals that can be made on this pinboard. Record them on dotted paper.

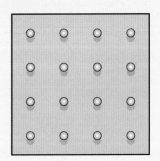

On a 4 × 4 pinboard, make two quadrilaterals. If they touch, or overlap, what new shapes can you see there?

I can recognise quadrilaterals

Shape properties

Some children made shaped name labels.
Write the shape of each label.
Choose from the shapes given.

1. quadrilateral

quadrilateral	triangle	pentagon

1
Katie

2
Steven

3
Sarah

4
Jenny

5
Gary

6
Mel

7
Kareem

8
Becky

9
Ben

hexagon	octagon	heptagon

Which of the shapes:

10 have sides that are all equal?

11 are symmetrical?

12 are quadrilaterals but not rectangles?

10. 3, 5 . . .

Draw four different quadrilaterals. Explain what is the same about them all, and what is different.

True or false?

1 A square is a quadrilateral.

2 A heptagon has one more side than a hexagon.

3 A triangle has half the number of sides of a hexagon.

4 An octagon has six corners.

5 A pentagon has one more side than a quadrilateral.

6 A quadrilateral can have an odd number of sides.

Write one true and one false statement about shapes.

7 Write the names of shapes a to g.

7. (a) pentagon

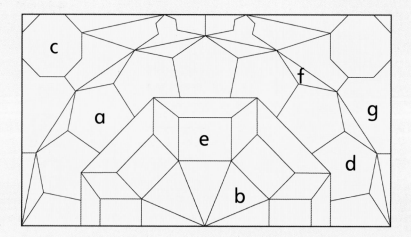

Draw your own pattern of shapes that fit together.

I can talk about the properties of 2D shapes

Prisms

Describe the faces of each prism.

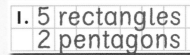

1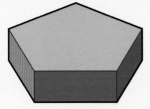

2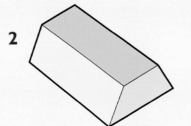

3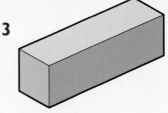

4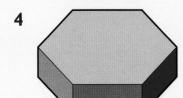

5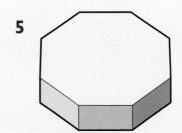

6

7   Copy and complete this table.

Prism	Faces
Triangular prism	5
Quadrilateral prism	
Pentagonal prism	
Hexagonal prism	
Heptagonal prism	
Octagonal prism	

8   What do you notice about each kind of prism and its number of faces?

I have a prism with 12 faces. How many sides does its end-face have?

I can talk about the faces of 3D objects

3D objects

a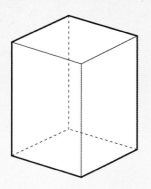

b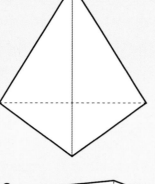

c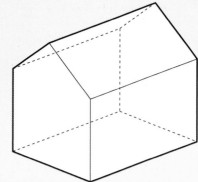

d

e

f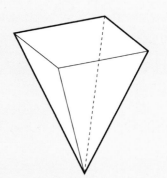

1 Copy and complete these tables.

shape				a		
faces	4	5	5	6	7	8

shape	b					
edges	6	8	9	12	15	18

shape		f				
vertices	4	5	6	8	10	12

Which of these shapes has a vertex where more than 3 edges meet? Try to make another shape from modelling dough with a vertex where more than 3 edges meet.

I can talk about the faces of 3D objects

True or false?

1. True

1   A cone has a circular face.

2   A cuboid has six vertices.

3   A pyramid has triangular faces.

4   A cylinder has no vertices.

5   A cube and a cuboid have equal numbers of edges.

6   A cylinder is a type of prism.

7   All pyramids have the same number of faces.

8   A cuboid only has rectangular faces.

9   Shapes with curved faces only begin with the letter 'c'.

10 A triangular pyramid has the same number of faces as a cube.

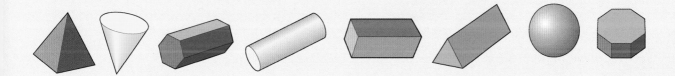

Make up some true and false statements about 3D objects for your partner to check.

11 Choose one of the shapes above and describe it to your partner, but do not name it.

Can they point to the shape you mean?

Copy each shape, then draw
any lines of symmetry.

1.

1 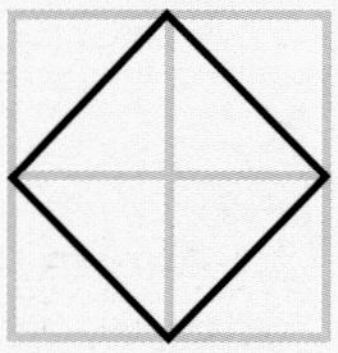   2 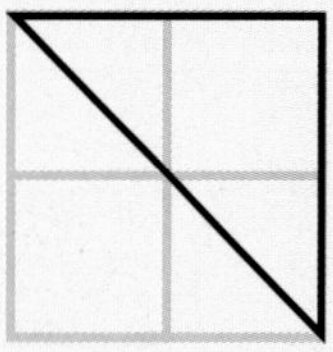   3 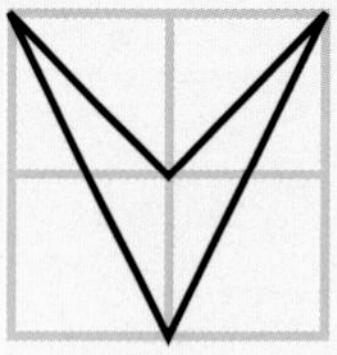   4

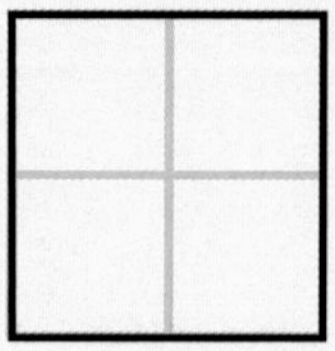

5 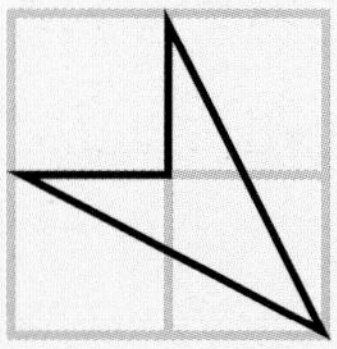   6 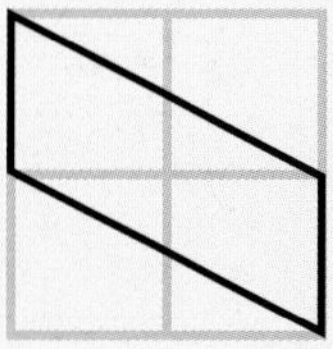   7 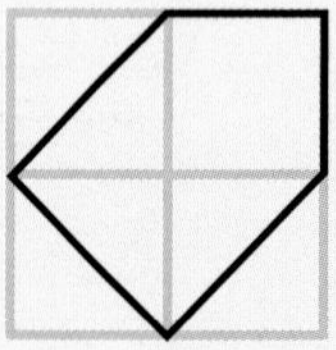   8

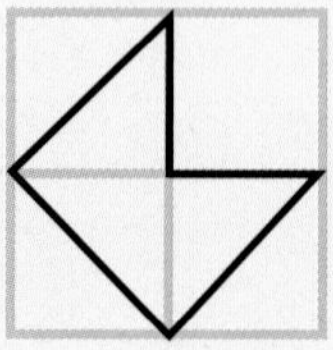

9 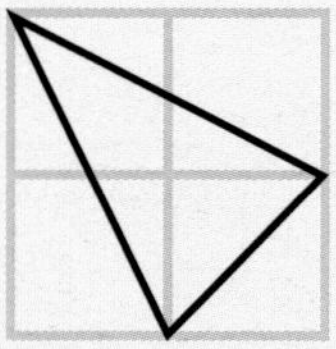   10 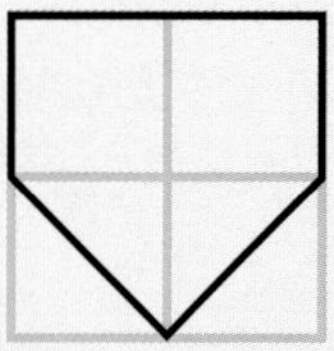   11 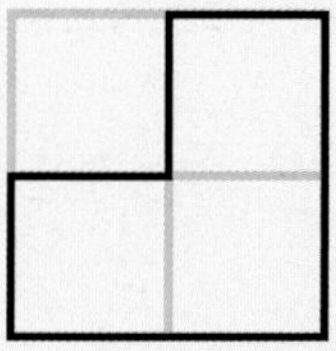   12

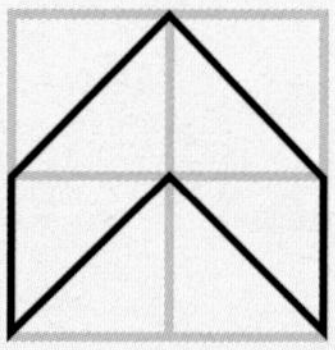

13 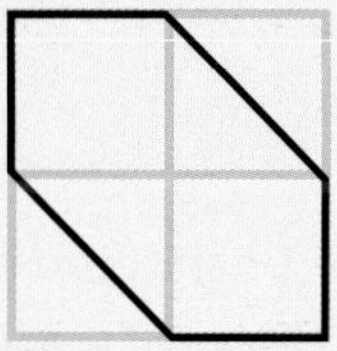 14 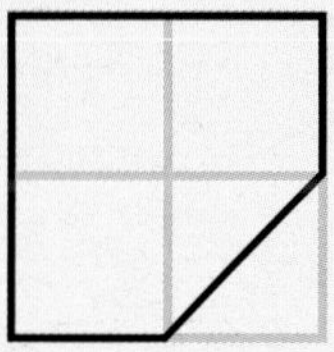 15 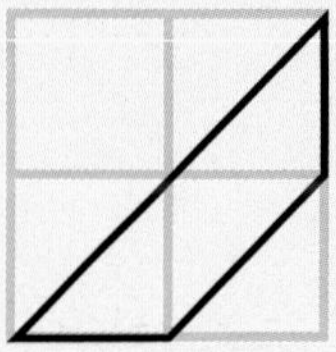 16

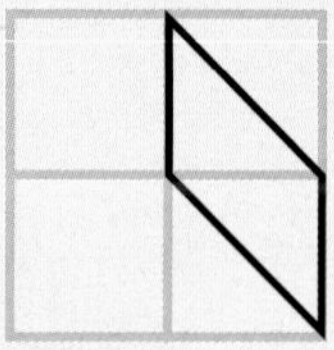

17 How many lines of symmetry are there in the letters of the
name CLAIRE?

CLAIRE

18 Investigate your name and your friends' names.

Write a word in capital letters where
every letter has one line of symmetry.

I can find lines of symmetry

Lines of symmetry

Check the lines of symmetry by laying a pencil or the edge of a ruler along each shape. Then write how many lines of symmetry each shape has.

1. 3

1

2

3

4

5

6

7

8

9

10 Choose a shape to copy, then draw its lines of symmetry.

Design your own symmetrical pattern.

Lines of symmetry

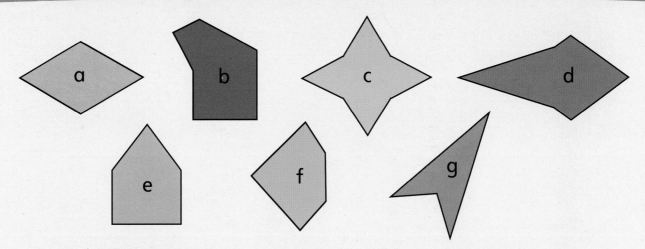

1 Draw 2 shapes of your own and label them h and i.
2 Copy and complete the table.

	no lines of symmetry	1 line of symmetry	2 lines of symmetry	3 lines of symmetry	more than 3 lines of symmetry
a			✓		
b					
c					
d					
e					
f					
g					
h					
i					

I can sort shapes according to their lines of symmetry

North, South, East, West

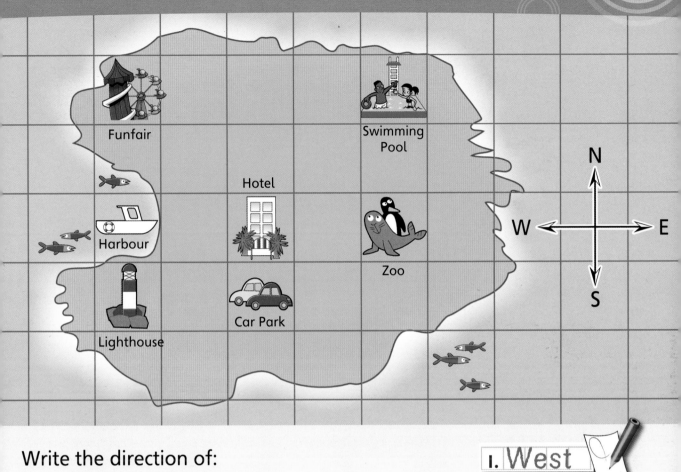

Write the direction of:

1. West

1 Harbour from Hotel

2 Zoo from Hotel

3 Lighthouse from Harbour

4 Swimming Pool from Funfair

5 Car Park from Hotel

6 Hotel from Car Park

7 Harbour from Zoo

8 Zoo from Swimming Pool

9 Look again at Question 1. You need to walk back to the Hotel from the Harbour. Which direction do you go in? Repeat this for the other questions.

Draw your own island on squared paper. Choose two places, then ask your partner to write the direction from one to the other.

I can write directions using the 4 compass points

North, South, East, West

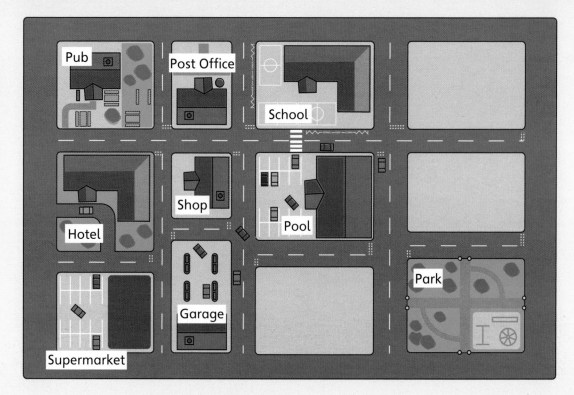

Write the direction if travelling from:

1. East

The Shop to:	**1** Pool	**2** Garage	**3** Hotel
The Post Office to:	**4** Pub	**5** School	**6** Garage
The Garage to:	**7** Park	**8** Post Office	**9** Supermarket

Describe two directions to go from:

10. East, South

10 Pub to Shop via Post Office

11 Garage to Hotel via Supermarket

Describe a journey to visit all the places on the map.

I can write directions using the 4 compass points

North, South, East, West

N

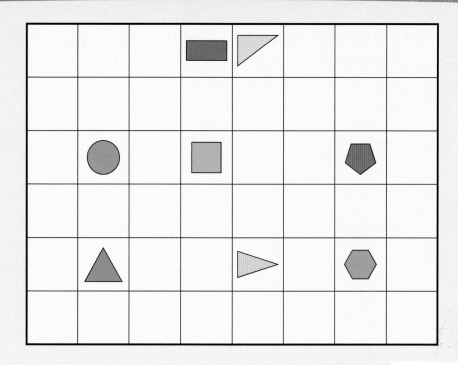

Draw the shape which is:

1 North of 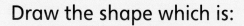	2 South of	3 East of
4 West of	5 South of	6 East of
7 West of	8 North of	9 East of

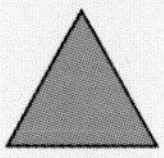

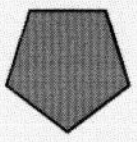

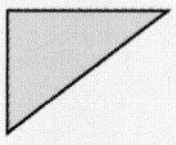

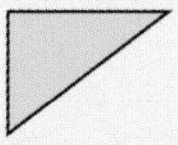

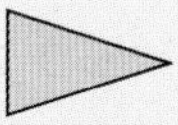

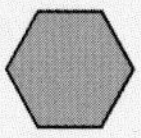

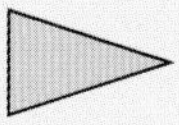

10 2 squares South of  ⬤ then 3 squares East

11 4 squares North of ▷ then 1 square West

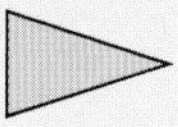

Make up more problems like Questions 10 and 11 for your partner to answer.

I can follow directions involving the 4 compass points

Right angles

Give the number of right angles through which the pointer has turned each time.

1. I right angle

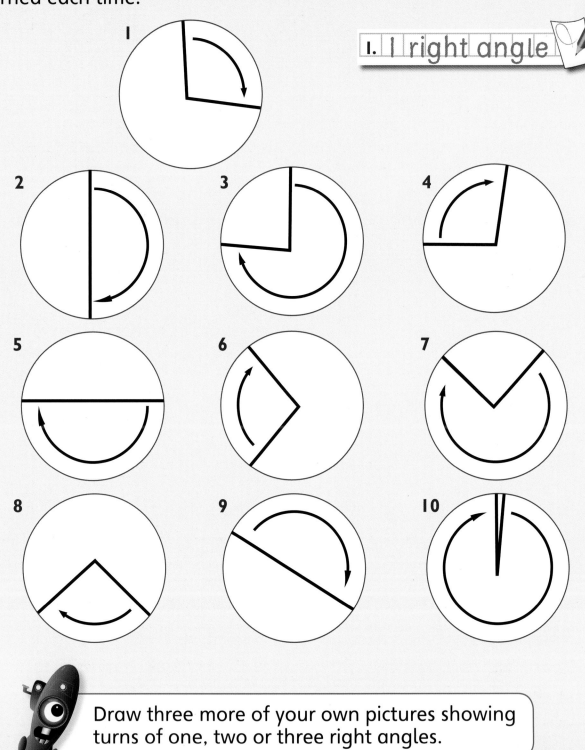

Draw three more of your own pictures showing turns of one, two or three right angles.

I can recognise turns made from one or more right angles

Turning

What number does the minute hand point to after these turns?

1

clockwise
I right angle

2

anticlockwise
2 right angles

3

clockwise
3 right angles

4

clockwise
2 right angles

5

anticlockwise
I right angle

6

clockwise
2 right angles

 I start at II. One clockwise right angle turn takes me to 2. How else could I have got there? Describe the turns.

True or false?

7 If you turn clockwise through I right angle you face the same direction as turning anticlockwise through 3 right angles.

8 If you make a three-quarter turn clockwise, you face the same direction as turning anticlockwise through 2 right angles.

9 If you turn anticlockwise through 5 right angles you face the same direction as turning anticlockwise through I right angle.

10 In 5 minutes the minute hand of a clock turns through one-third of a right angle.

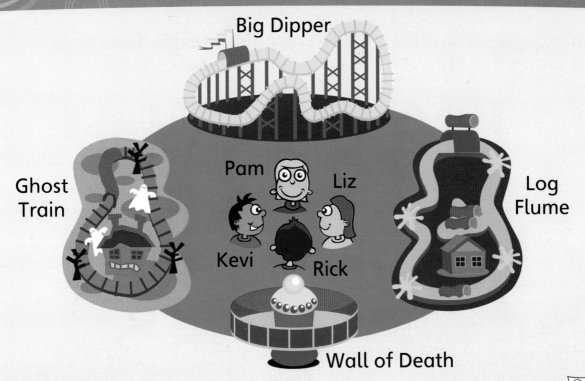

Big Dipper

Ghost Train

Pam

Liz

Kevi

Rick

Log Flume

Wall of Death

Write the ride that each child will face after these turns:

1. Ghost Train

Rick:

1 clockwise, 3 right angles
2 anticlockwise, 2 right angles

Liz:

3 anticlockwise, 1 right angle
4 clockwise, 3 right angles

Kevi:

5 clockwise, 2 right angles
6 anticlockwise, 1 right angle

Pam:

7 anticlockwise, 4 right angles
8 clockwise, 5 right angles

9 Rick's first turn leaves him facing the Ghost Train. How else could he have turned to face the same way? Repeat for the other children's first turns too.

Design your own theme park! Write instructions like those above and ask your partner to answer the questions.

I can make and describe right angle turns

Work with your partner. Take turns to describe out loud the turns along this route. Use the words 'right angle', 'clockwise' and 'anticlockwise'.

Find a quick way to record these turns and write them out.

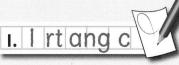

I. I rt ang c

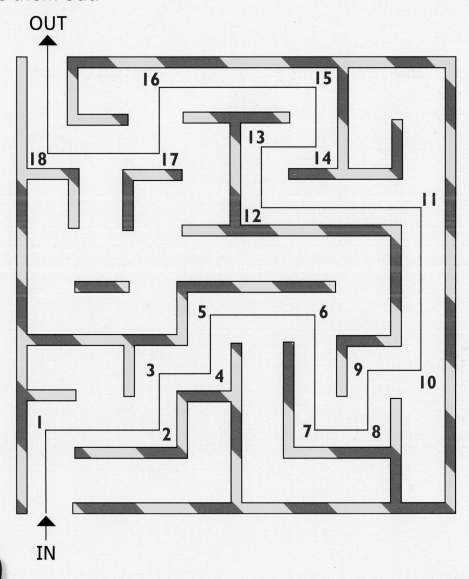

OUT

16   15
        13
18   17   14
        12   11
        5   6
    3   4   9
                10
    I   2   7   8

IN

Find another way through the maze. Record the route using your shorthand. Can your partner use your instructions to find your route through the maze?

 I can describe right angle turns

Use a clockface. Describe, in right angles, these clockwise turns of the minute hand.

I.2 right angles

1
From: half past 7
To: 8 o'clock

2
From: quarter to 1
To: half past 1

3
From: ten past 3
To: twenty-five past 3

4
From: five past 6
To: ten to 7

5
From: five to 4
To: ten past 4

6
From: twenty-five to 10
To: five past 10

7
From: 5 o'clock
To: quarter past 5

8
From: 8 o'clock
To: 9 o'clock

Write your own 'from' and 'to' for the minute hand to turn through:

9 3 right angles

10 2 right angles

11 1 right angle

12 4 right angles

Describe some before and after times where the hour hand moves through 1 right angle.

Angles

For each turn, write 'less than', 'more than' or 'equal to' a right angle.

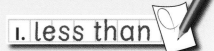

1

2

3

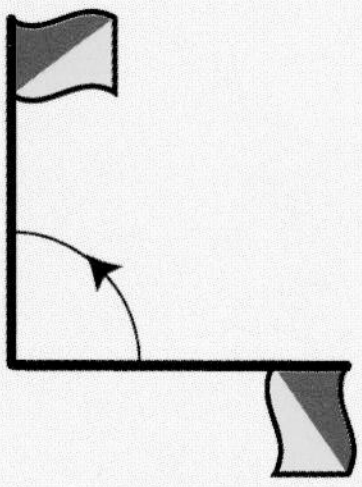

4

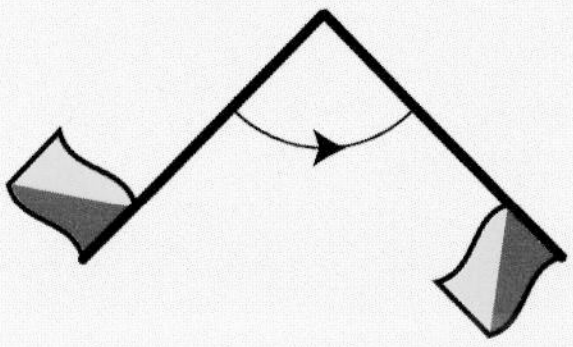

5

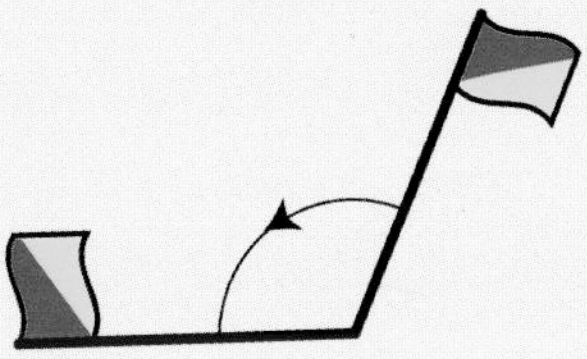

6

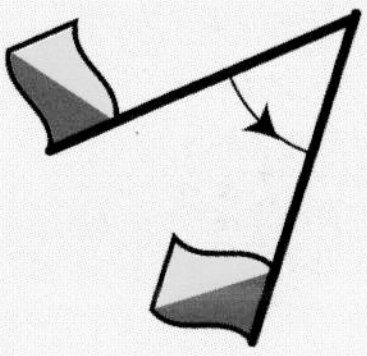

For each angle marked, write 'less than', 'more than' or 'equal to' a right angle.

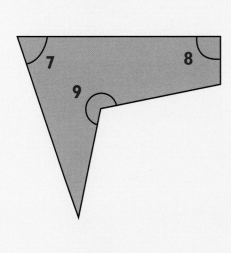

7   8

9

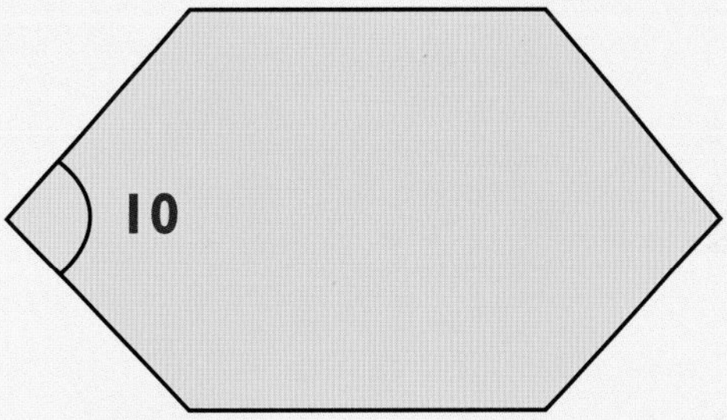

10

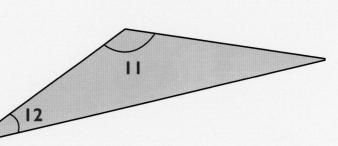

11

12

Draw a 2D shape with 5 right angles.
Draw one with no right angles.

I can say whether an angle is larger, smaller or equal to a right angle

37

Shape angles

Count the number of right angles in each shape.

1

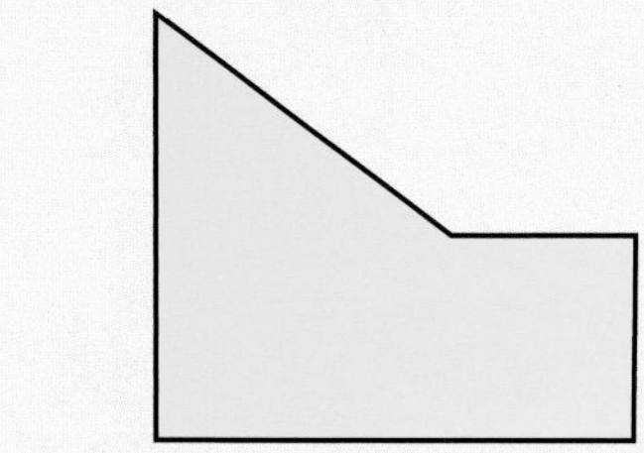

2

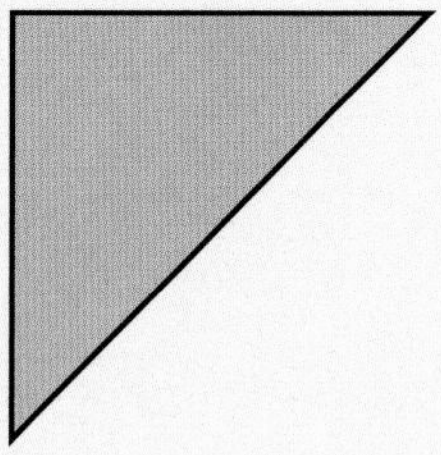

3

4

5

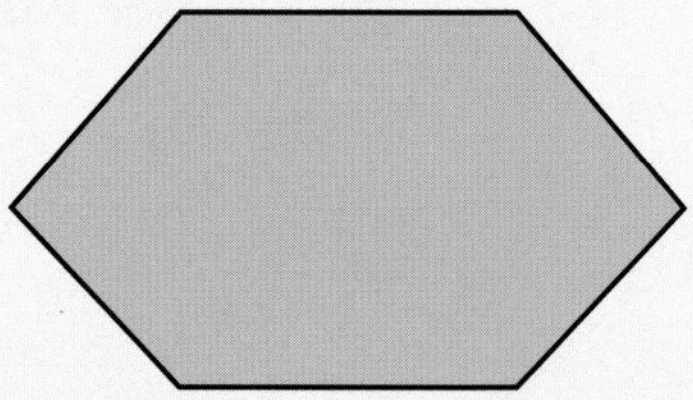

6

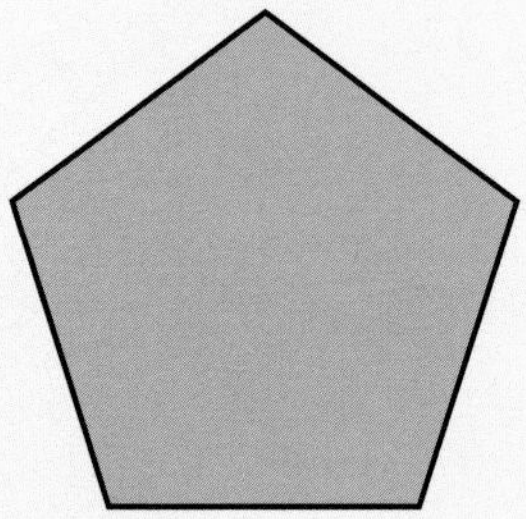

7

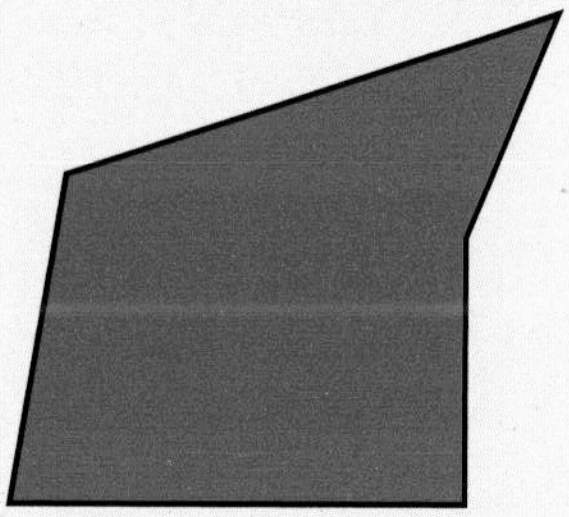

8

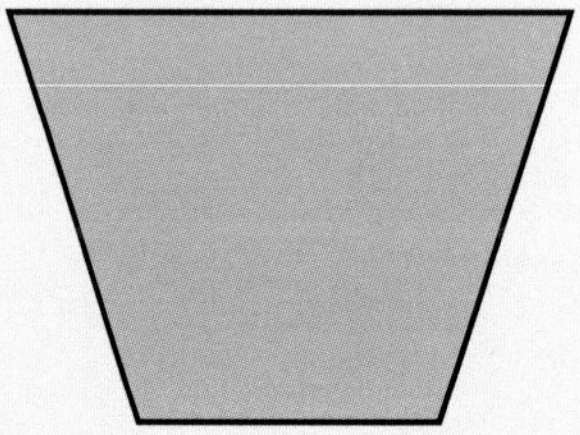

9

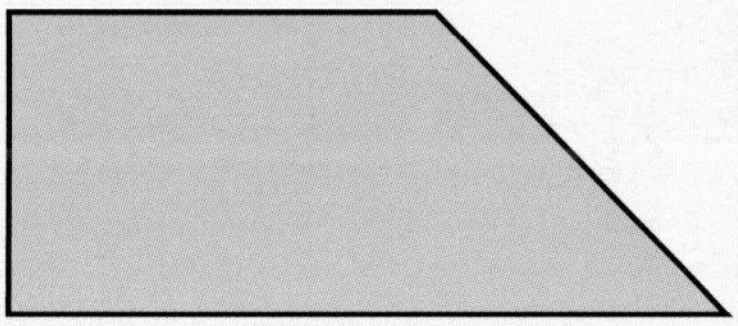

10

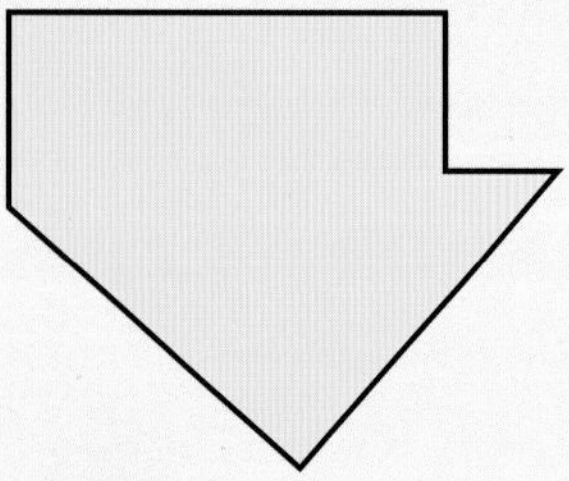

11

12

Can you draw a pentagon with exactly 3 right angles?

I can count the number of right angles in a 2D shape

Giving directions

This map shows a park with a lake in it.

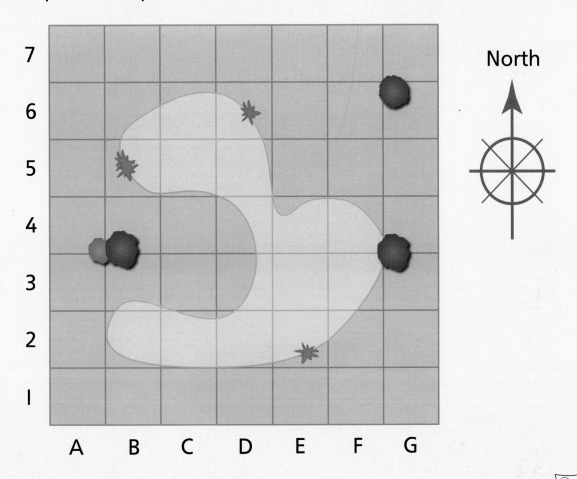

North

Write how to get from square
to square avoiding the lake.

1. West 2, North 2

1 From C4 to A6   2   From E5 to E1

3 From C3 to E6   4   From F5 to A2   5 From D1 to C4

6 Make up three journeys like this, for a boat on the lake.

Write how to make a journey right round the lake.

We would like to say a special thanks to all of the children who entered our design a character competition, and congratulations to our winners!

Character designed by Olivia Ferry, age 10
St Matthew's Primary School, Glasgow
Stylish Seahorse

Interpretation of the winning design by
Volker Beisler (professional illustrator)

Author Team:
Lynda Keith, Hilary Koll and Steve Mills

Published by Pearson Education Limited, Edinburgh Gate, Harlow, Essex, CM20 2JE.

www.pearsonschools.co.uk

Text © Pearson Education Limited 2011

Typeset by Debbie Oatley @ room9design
Illustrations © Harcourt Education Limited 2006-2007, Pearson Education Limited 2011
Illustrated by Piers Baker, John Haslam, Nigel Kitching, Mark Ruffle, Eric Smith, Andrew Hennessey, Gary Swift, Andy Hammond, Matt Buckley, Seb Burnett, Debbie Oatley, Jim Peacock, Dave Williams, Chris Winn, Anthony Rule, Annabel Tempest, Glen McBeth
Cover design by Pearson Education Limited
Cover illustration Volker Beisler © Pearson Education Limited
Printed in Malaysia, CTP-KHL

The authors Lynda Keith, Hilary Koll and Steve Mills assert their moral right to be identified as the authors of this work.

First published 2011

15 14 13 12 11
10 9 8 7 6 5 4 3 2

British Library Cataloguing in Publication Data
A catalogue record for this book is available from the British Library

ISBN 978 0 435 04785 6

Acknowledgements
Every effort has been made to contact copyright holders of material reproduced in this book.
Any omissions will be rectified in subsequent printings if notice is given to the publishers.